WESTERN
SCROLL SAW AND INLAY PATTERNS

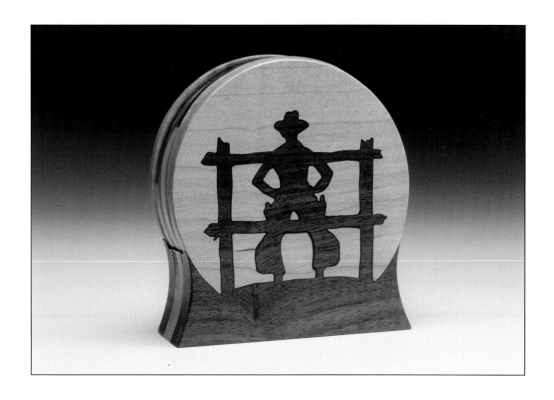

By Joe and Paige Paisley

D1530686

FOX BOOKS
Fox Chapel Publishing Co Inc.

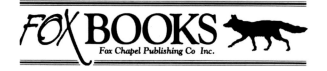

CLINTON PUBLIC LIBRARY
CLINTON, IOWA
52732

Copyright © 1999 Fox Chapel Publishing Company Inc. The patterns contained herein are copyrighted by the author. Artists may make three copies of these patterns for personal use and may make any number of projects based on these patterns. The patterns themselves, however, are not to be duplicated for resale or distribution under any circumstances. Any such copying is a violation of copyright laws.

Publisher: Alan Giagnocavo
Project Editor: Ayleen Stellhorn
Desktop Specialist: Linda L. Eberly, Eberly Designs Inc.
Interior Photography: Carl Shuman, Owl Hill Studios
Cover Photography: Carl Shuman, Owl Hill Studios

ISBN # 1-56523-118-X

To order your copy of this book,
please send check or money order
for $14.95 plus $2.50 shipping to:
Fox Books
1970 Broad Street
East Petersburg, PA 17520

Manufactured in Korea

1495

Table of Contents

CLINTON PUBLIC LIBRARY
CLINTON, IOWA
52732

FOREWORD

We would like to dedicate this to our moms, Anita and Arlyne, for their great support. From the beginning, even for the times when we were on the wrong road, their strength and patience prevailed to show us, yes you can do this. Thanks moms.

It is very easy for us to design and build one-of-a-kind pieces; this is a daily thing for us. But writing a foreword is something that can be a real hurdle if you have never written one before. I suppose we should give you reasons why we are doing this book, what it can do for you and what brought us to this point.

We wrote this book to give you some patterns that you may not have been able to get and to expose you to some techniques you may not have learned yet. Wyoming gives us some very beautiful sights, sounds and inspirations that overwhelm us to draw, design and create, so we would like to share them with you.

What can these designs do for you? Well for us it has added a whole new flare, dimension and wow to our furniture, lighting and other projects. Hopefully it will give you a new dimension to your one-of-a-kind pieces, show you how easy inlays can be and how flexible they are.

What brought us to this point? First, the fun and freedom of creating. Second, other woodcrafters asking us to create new patterns and projects for them. And third, clients that demand creativity and one-of-a-kind pieces for their homes, lodges and offices.

We would like to add one more item. Thank you to our families and friends for their patience, RB Industries for their great support, Fox Chapel Publishing for taking us on sight unseen, Woodworkers Supply for being good friends, and our banker Candy for being there for us through thick and thin. And to our three boys.... Thanks! To Josh, for your woodworking imagination — yeah, that will work; to Matt that it is important to take time off and go fishing; and to Daren, well bud, woodworking is a real job.

Good luck,
Joe and Paige Paisley

MAGNETS

These cowboy magnets provide a simple project for the beginning scroll saw artist. Advanced scrollers may want to use this pattern for a quick project. For professional woodworkers, these magnets are a great moneymaker. Cut out four magnets every 30 minutes and sell them at your next craft show for $3 each. Your potential is unlimited. Many of the patterns in this book can be used to make magnets. Try the hats on page 52 or the cows on page 85.

WOOD
Walnut is pictured here, but many woods will work. You may want to take the color of the refrigerator into consideration when choosing your wood.

MATERIALS LIST—MAGNETS

- 4 layers of $1/8$" walnut or any wood of your choice
- 4 sticky-back magnet sheets cut to the same size as the wood
- 4 dowels: – $1/4$" diameter, 1" long
- clamps
- pattern cut to fit the wood
- spray mount adhesive
- 1 – $15/64$" drill bit
- sandpaper or electric sander
- 1 drill bit sized larger than your scroll saw blade
- spray finish
- scroll saw with #2-#5 blade

1   Peel the backing off the magnet sheets. Adhere the sticky side of the magnet sheets to the back of the wood. Put magnet sheets on each of the four pieces of wood. Make sure the backing covers the entire area that the pattern will cover.

2   Layer the wood in a stack, one piece on top of the other with the magnet side down. Clamp the wood together tightly with pony clamps and use spray adhesive to apply the pattern to the wood. Because of the added thickness of the magnetic backing, you will only be able to cut four pieces of wood at one time.

3   Drill one hole in each corner of the stack of wood with the $15/64$" drill bit and insert the $1/4$" dowels into the holes. The dowels will keep the wood in the stack from sliding as you use the scroll saw and force the wood to lay flat on the scroll saw table.

With the wood securely in place, drill a starting holes for your inside cuts. Use a drill bit that is slightly larger than your scroll saw blade.

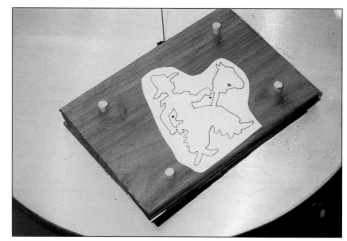

4   Drill three holes for inside cuts: one under the cowboy's right arm, one under his left arm and one under the horse's neck. These holes will provide a starting point for removing wood from the inside cuts.

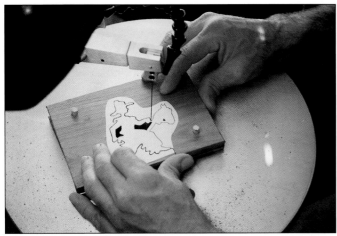

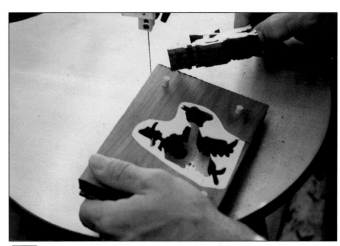

5 | Always cut in the center of your pattern and work your way out. I cut out the wood under the cowboy's left arm first. Then I removed the piece under his right arm. Next I will cut the pattern outline.

6 | When all three pieces are cut out, remove the cowboy and peel the paper off the wood. A damp cloth will help to remove the paper from the wood.

7 | Separate the magnets and sand the pieces as needed. Remove the dust with a tack cloth or air hose and finish the pieces with a 30-minute polyurethane spray or another finishing product of your choice.

Notice how one of the cowboys in this photo is facing in the opposite direction? I purposely made him face the other way by stacking that one piece of wood with the magnet side up instead of down.

©1999 Paige Paisley

Pine Candle Shelf

This pine candle shelf makes a nice addition to any room. The green background, the red ribbon and the gold paint on the edges give the piece in this photo a holiday look. Try using different colors to make your shelf unique.

MATERIALS LIST—SHELF
- 3 piece of clear or knotty pine
- shelf back: $3/4$" thick, 8" wide, $13^3/4$" long
- shelf: $3/4$" thick, $3^1/2$" wide, 8" long
- candle: $3/8$" thick, 8" wide, 12" long
- pattern
- wood glue
- 1" screws
- sandpaper or electric sander
- acrylic paint
- clear, non-yellowing sealer

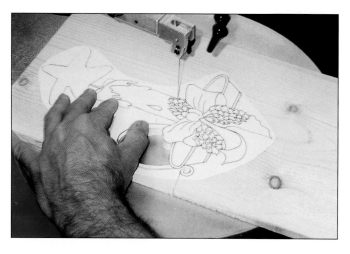

When you have chosen the colors you like, start by painting the candle piece first. After it is completely painted, center it between the top of the shelf back and the shelf and glue it to the shelf back. Do not paint the back side of the candle. If you do, the adhesive bond between the candle and the shelf back will not be very strong and the piece will soon fall off. Paint the shelf back and the shelf with the colors you chose. I used a sponge to apply gold paint to the the edges of my shelf. When the piece is dry, apply a clear non-yellowing sealer.

Apply the pattern to the wood with spray adhesive. Using a band saw, cut out the shelf and the shelf back. You may want to router the edges of the shelf for a more decorative look. Fit the shelf to the shelf back and mark the drilling holes for the screws. Next glue the shelf to the shelf back. Screws ensure that the shelf will stay put.

Now onto the scrolling. First, drill a starting hole inside the handle of the candle holder and remove that piece. This piece can be discarded. Next cut out the rest of the piece. Note that you will be cutting only on the outside line of the entire piece. The pine cone, bow and details on the candle are painting references.

Sand all three pieces—the shelf back, the shelf and the candle—and use a tack cloth to remove any dust. Apply a clear sealer, and you're ready to paint.

Use any colors you like to paint this project or you may choose to stain it. I used acrylic paints to finish the piece pictured in this chapter.

©1999 Paige Paisley

Shelf

Top

Bottom

Inlaid Card Holder

Two pieces of contrasting wood cut at the same time make this inlaid card holder a beautiful way to keep cards and other papers organized. Use the techniques in this demonstration and other patterns in this book (or your own design) to create different card holders.

WOOD
Walnut (for the dark pieces) and spalted maple (for the light pieces) were used in this piece. Any two contrasting woods will work well. If you choose spalted wood, be sure to use a mask or respirator as the wood dust may pose a serious health hazard.

MATERIALS LIST—CARD HOLDER

- 2 layers of 3/8" wood, preferably contrasting colors
- spray mount
- clamps
- 4 dowels: 1/4" diameter, 1" long
- pattern cut to fit the wood
- 15/64" drill bit
- 1 drill bit sized larger than your scroll saw blade
- sandpaper or electric sander
- spray finish
- tray to hold the cut-out pieces
- 2" clear tape
- clear epoxy
- acrylic paint to match the darkest wood color

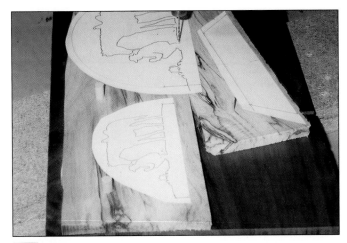

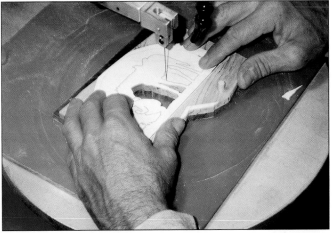

1 | Choose two pieces of contrasting wood. I am using spalted maple and walnut for this demonstration. Layer the pieces of wood, clamp them together and apply the pattern with spray adhesive. Drill holes to fit the 1/4" dowels. Insert the dowels; then remove the clamps.

Drill a starter hole for your scroll saw blade in an area of the pattern where it won't be noticeable when the pieces are reassembled. I chose the corner of the pattern where the cowboy's heel is touching the ground for the first piece to be removed.

2 | When cutting inlaid projects such as this one, set your table for zero clearance so you don't lose any of the pieces. Cut the inside pieces of the pattern first. I start with the piece between the cowboy and the horse, and then move to the areas between the horse's legs and the small areas under the coffee pot and inside the handle. As you remove the inside pieces, place them in a tray next to your table. Next, cut the outer half-circle. Your final cut should be along the outline of the piece.

Now cut out the smaller cowboy and horse pattern. When cutting out this part of the project, you need not save the inside cut pieces or the outer piece of wood. You'll also want to cut out the base at this time.

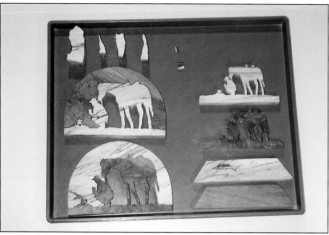

3 | Now you need to mix your pieces. Because you cut the pattern from two pieces of wood, you'll have enough pieces to make two complete projects. For one piece, I use the walnut for the background and the spalted maple for the picture itself. The smaller cowboy and horse and the base cut from spalted maple will complete this piece. The second piece is reversed, with the spalted maple forming the background.

4 | Apply two-inch-wide clear tape to one side of the piece to hold everything in place. Turn the piece over. Mix clear epoxy with sawdust from the project or with acrylic paint that matches the darker wood color. Apply the colored epoxy to the surface forcing it into the cut lines. Keep the layer of the epoxy thin; it will be easier to sand. Let the piece dry and sand it with 150-grit sandpaper to remove any excess epoxy. Peel off the tape and apply the colored epoxy to the other side of the piece. Let the epoxy dry and sand the piece. A second light coat of epoxy may be necessary if air pockets or settling has occurred. The epoxy will hold the project together and give you clean-looking lines.

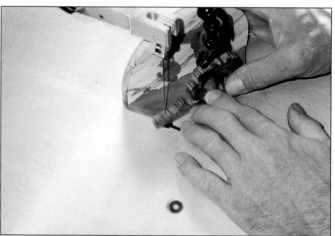

5 | Glue and clamp the front piece, base and back piece together with wood glue. Let the project dry overnight.

6 | When the glue is dry, cut away the excess wood on the front of the card holder. Sand the bottom and all the edges smooth. Use tack cloth to remove any remaining dust and then use a spray finish or a finish of your choice to complete your project.

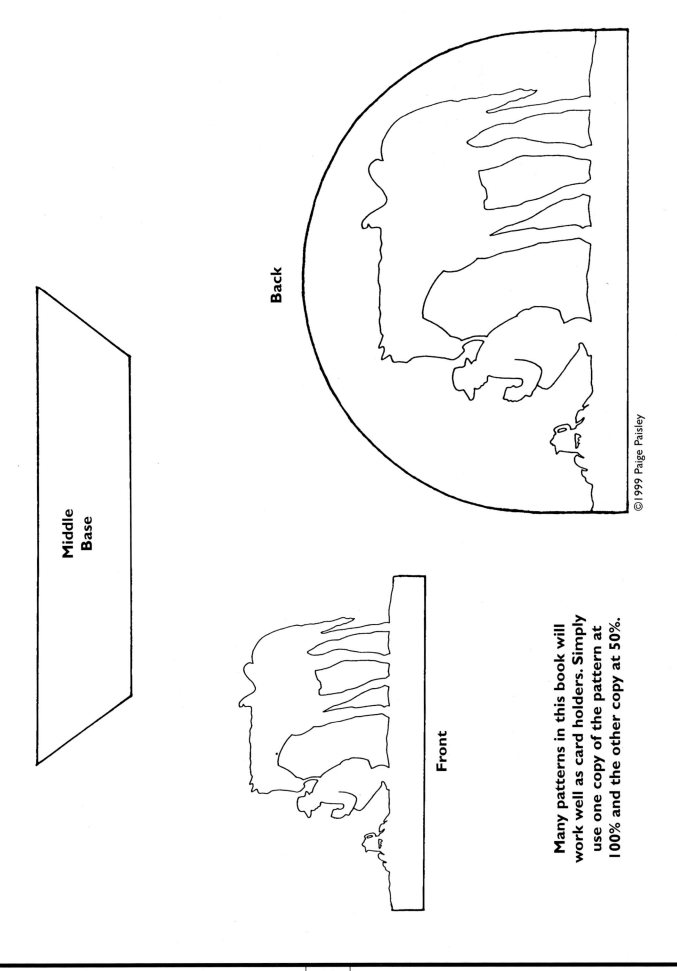

**Middle
Base**

Back

© 1999 Paige Paisley

Front

Many patterns in this book will work well as card holders. Simply use one copy of the pattern at 100% and the other copy at 50%.

Inlaid Coasters

These inlaid coasters come with their own rack. Mix and match patterns and wood to create a special place upon which to rest a drink.

WOOD

Maple was used for the light-colored pieces and walnut for the dark-colored pieces in these two coasters. Any two woods that have a nice contrast in color work well for coasters.

MATERIALS LIST—COASTERS

- 2 pieces of $1/4$"-thick wood, preferably contrasting colors
- 4 dowels: $1/4$" diameter, 1" long
- $15/64$" bit
- hammer
- 1 drill bit slightly larger than a #2 blade
- spray mount
- tray for wood pieces
- clear epoxy
- walnut-colored acrylic paint
- sandpaper
- 2" clear tape
- clamps
- finish of choice

Place the pattern on one piece of wood, then stack and clamp the pieces of wood together. Drill one pilot hole in each corner with the $15/64$" bit. Hammer the $1/4$" dowels into the pilot holes to hold the layers of wood in place.

Drill starter holes for the scroll saw blade in inconspicuous places along the pattern lines. All inside pieces must be saved, so do not drill starter holes in the center of the inside pieces.

Using a #2 scroll saw blade in your saw, cut out the pieces. Start with the inside pieces; cut the outer circle last.

Place all the pattern pieces on a tray. Remember that it is important to keep your pieces in order for reassembly. When all the pieces are cut, mix and match the pieces to form two coasters and four base pieces.

To make a complete set, as shown above and on page 14, you'll need to cut two coasters of each of the three designs on pages 15 and 16 and six base pieces. Two of the six coasters and all six base pieces will be used to form the rack for the other four coasters. One cowboy coaster and one cowgirl coaster were used to make the rack in the picture.

When all the inlay pieces are assembled, apply clear tape to one side of the coasters to hold the pieces in place. Mix the epoxy with a small amount of walnut-colored acrylic paint. Turn the coasters over and work the tinted epoxy into the cuts between the inlay pieces. Let the epoxy dry and then sand the coasters. If necessary, apply another coat of tinted epoxy to fill in any remaining air holes. Let the epoxy dry and sand the coaster again. Turn the coaster over, remove the tape and repeat the epoxy steps on the other side of the coasters.

Glue the four base bottoms together, let the glue dry and sand. Sanding must be done now, because you can't sand the center of the base after you glue on the outsides. Glue the outsides to the center, making sure everything is lined up, clamp and let dry. Sand all the pieces, then apply a durable finish.

©1999 Paige Paisley

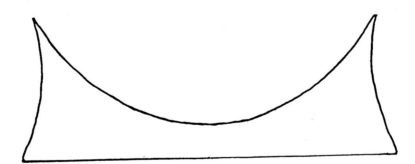

Base

©1999 Paige Paisley

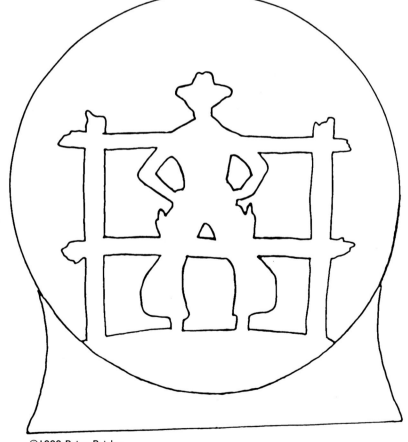

©1999 Paige Paisley

Santa Christmas Ornament

Six different shades of wood are cut at once to give these Western-style Santa ornaments a uniquely varied look. When finished, these ornaments can be used on their own or turned into inlays for wooden boxes. Let your imagination run wild.

WOOD

Scrap wood from cabinet shops will give you a wide variety of woods to choose from at a fraction of the cost. Try any combination of the following:

Maple: light, even color.
Spalted maple: light color with dark streaks. (Be sure to use a ventilator or mask when working with this wood as the dust may be a health hazard.)
Australian lace wood: reddish in color.
Purple heart: purple colored.
Walnut: dark with a very straight grain.
Burled walnut: a dark, highly figured wood.
Babanga: tan in color.

MATERIALS LIST—ORNAMENT

- 6 different woods, each $1/8$" thick
- clamps
- pattern
- spray adhesive
- sandpaper or electric sander
- $15/64$" drill bit
- 1 drill bit sized larger than your scroll saw blade
- 4 dowels: $1/4$" diameter, 1" long
- tack cloth
- spray finish
- zero clearance table
- tray to hold cut pieces

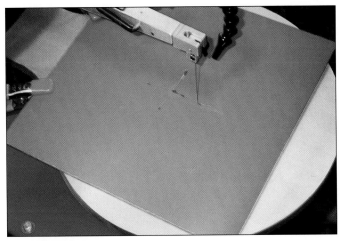

1 | Because this is an inlay project, use a zero clearance table. Use a #2 blade or a blade that works well in your scroll saw. Don't forget to have a tray close by to put all the inlay pieces in after they've been cut out. As you cut, try to keep your pieces in order. Remember, all of the pieces will be saved for this inlaid ornament.

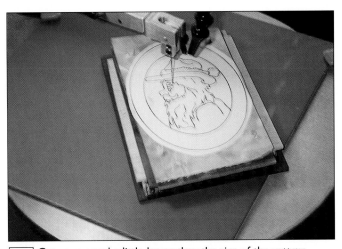

2 | Cut your wood a little larger than the size of the pattern. Stack all six pieces of wood and apply the pattern to the top piece of wood with spray adhesive. (If six pieces of wood is too many for you to cut, try using only three or four different pieces.) Clamp the wood together, then drill holes in each corner with the $15/64$" bit and hammer in the dowels. Now drill holes for the inside cuts. Because you are saving all the pieces for inlay, be sure to place the starter holes in inconspicuous spots. Start with the inside cuts and work your way out.

3 | After the pieces are cut out and placed in the tray, begin putting your pieces together by intermixing the colors. You may only end up with three or four ornaments that you feel will work, but stack cutting is still faster than cutting one ornament at a time. Place 2" clear tape on one side of the ornament to hold the pieces together. Flip the ornament over and apply clear epoxy mixed with saw dust or acrylic paint to the wood. Use your fingers (rubber gloves are a big help here) to work the colored epoxy into the cracks of the ornaments. Let the epoxy dry, then remove the tape and repeat the process on the other side. Sand the ornaments and apply a finish of your choice to the completed piece.

©1999 Paige Paisley

Santa Box

Use any of the patterns to create an inlay for the top of this box. Here, the Western-style Santa ornaments (page 18) are centered within a wreath of holly leaves and berries.

WOOD

Cherry was used for the leaves and maple for the background of the box pictured in the top photo. In the photograph to the right, the woods were reversed. The woods used for the Western-style Santa ornaments are listed on page 18.

MATERIALS LIST—SANTA BOX

- 2 colors of wood cut 10$\frac{1}{4}$" by 13" by $\frac{1}{4}$" thick for the lid and sides
- 2 pieces of wood 7 $\frac{1}{4}$" by 10" for the bottom
- 4 dowels: 1" diameter
- spray adhesive
- clamps
- $\frac{15}{64}$" drill bit
- 1 drill bit smaller than the scroll blade
- 2 trays to hold the inlay pieces
- rubber bands
- finish of your choice
- pattern
- epoxy
- acrylic paint

1 | Clamp the wood together. Drill holes in each corner of the wood with the 15/64" bit and insert the dowels. Drill a starter hole for the saw blade next to a leaf on the inside of the pattern.

2 | Start cutting the inside of the pattern first. After the inside has been cut, remove the center piece and place it on a nearby tray.

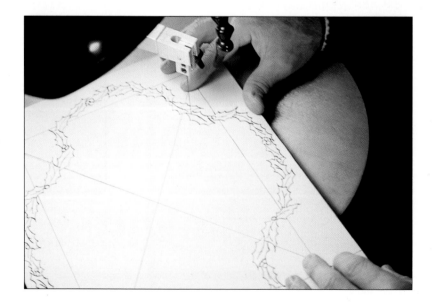

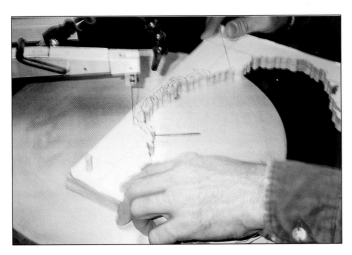

3 | Now begin cutting each leaf and berry, placing all the pieces back together in order on the tray. You may want to number each piece before you begin cutting.

4 | As you place each leaf and berry on the tray, mix the colors of wood pieces after each cut. For this demonstration, I'll end up with two box tops. Once has a leaf chain of cherry with maple berries and a maple background; the other has a leaf chain of maple with cherry berries and a cherry background. Use tape to hold the pieces together.

5 | Next, cut out the four doweled corners and replace the outside piece. This will be a tight fit. Tint epoxy with burnt umber paint and work the colored epoxy into the cracks. Let the epoxy dry and sand. Turn the piece over, remove the tape and repeat the epoxy step on the other side. You may need to repeat the epoxy and sanding steps another time to fill in any air holes remaining after the first application.

Mark the sides and the center of the piece with a pencil. Place the Santa inlay at the intersection of the center lines and trace around it.

6 | At this point, you have some options to make your box unique to your project. 1) You can use a router to router out space for your Santa inlay. Note that the Santa inlay is thinner than the box top, so router out only $1/8$" of wood to make the Santa inlay lay flat. 2) You could also cut out the hole with a scroll saw, then glue the Santa to the piece of wood you just cut out. Push the glued-together piece through until the top of the inlay is flush with the lid. Glue or epoxy around the edge of the cutout to hold it in place. Then sand off the back of the piece until it is flat against the inside of the lid. 3) You could simply round the edge of the Santa inlay and glue it on top of the box. (Instructions continue on page 26.)

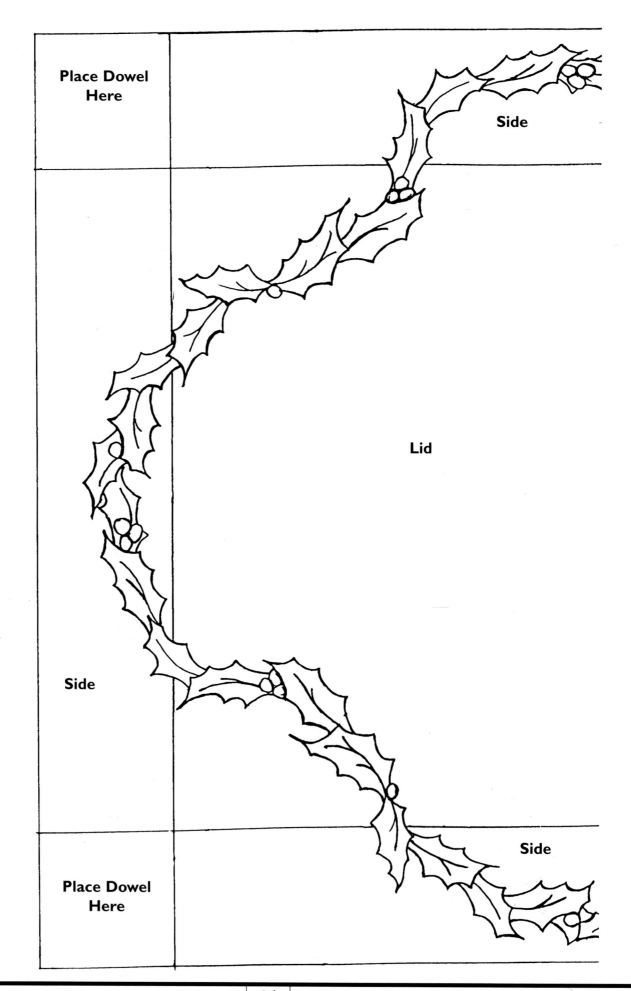

Place Dowel Here

Side

Lid

Side

Side

Place Dowel Here

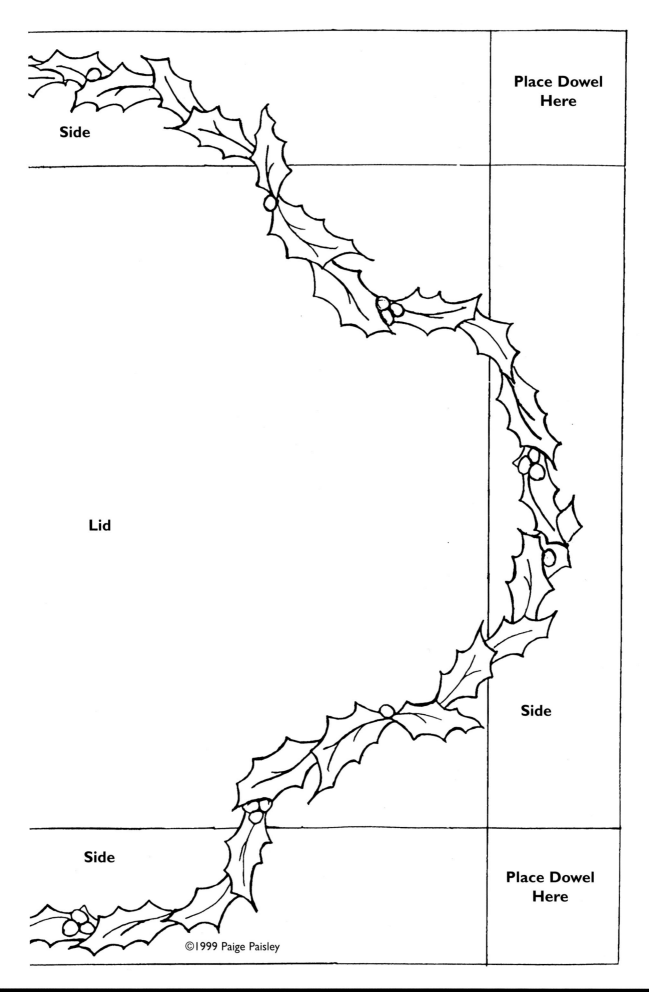

Side

Place Dowel
Here

Lid

Side

Side

Place Dowel
Here

©1999 Paige Paisley

CLINTON PUBLIC LIBRARY
CLINTON, IOWA
52732

7 | Now cut off the four sides of the box. Cut slowly because the epoxy is not as hard as the wood.

8 | Cut a 45-degree angle on each of the ends of the box sides. When you're ready to glue and assemble the sides and the base, a rubber band works well to clamp things in place.

9 | To make a lid for the box, you have two options.

Option #1 is to line the inside of the lid with wooden strips or a piece of solid wood. Option #1 must be done before putting the bottom on the box. Place the lid on the four sides, flip the box over and align the lid, then clamp the lid and the sides together. Cut four $1/4$" by $1/4$" strips or one solid piece of wood to fit on the inside of the box lid. Mark the inside of the box lid with a pencil, remove the clamps holding the lid and the sides together, and glue the four pieces or the one solid piece in place. To finish the box, take a $7 1/4$" piece of wood and clamp the four sides to the bottom. Use a sharp pencil to mark the inside of the box shape. Cut the bottom piece out and glue it to the inside of the four sides to form the bottom of the box. The lid lays on top of the finished box.

Option #2 is to add hinges to hold the lid in place. First make sure your box bottom is glued into place and dry. Now align the lid on the box top. Clamp the lid in place and mark the position of the hinges. Remember to allow for wood expansion.

With both options, round all the edges by sanding. This will give the effect of the leaves rolling over the sides of the box. Check all the inlay areas for any places that may need an additional application of epoxy. Do the final sanding and remove any dust with a tack cloth. Complete the piece with the finish of your choice.

Rustic Magazine Holder

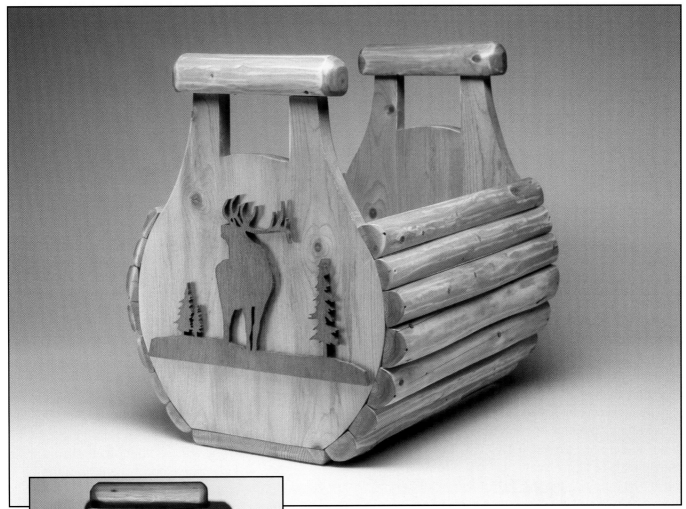

This magazine holder lends a beautiful touch to any room. The half-circle poles used to form the sides give it a rustic look. Try any of the patterns as cutouts or inlays for the ends.

WOOD
Any type of wood can be used for this piece. If you add a cutout or inlay on the end, be sure to pick woods that will create a striking contrast with the holder.

MATERIAL LIST—MAGAZINE HOLDER

- 1 – 16" by 6 $1/2$" by $3/4$" piece of wood for base
- 2 – 14" by 12" by $3/4$ " for ends
- 7 – 16" by 1 $1/2$" diameter poles or dowels
- 1 – 14" by 1 $1/2$" diameter poles or dowels for
- handles
- pattern for holder
- pattern for cutouts
- $1/8$" or $1/4$" wood for cutouts
- sandpaper or electric sander
- carpenters glue
- 2 different colors of stain, your choice
- 2" finish nails, approximately 40
- finish of choice
- hammer and nail punch
- tack cloth
- spray adhesive

Apply the patterns for the end and the base to the wood and cut those pieces out. Glue the ends of the magazine holder to the top of the base, let the glue dry, then turn the piece over and nail it together.

Next, take your seven poles or dowels, mark a centerline at the end of each pole, and slice each down the center. This will give you 14 half-circle poles, each 16" long. Nails will need to be driven into each half-circle pole $3/8$" in from each end. Pre-drill the holes now.

Start assembly on one side of the magazine rack by gluing and nailing the first half-circle pole in place; then glue and nail the first half-circle pole on the other side. Alternate back and forth between sides, repeating the process until you have applied al of the poles. This will stabilize and keep your magazine holder straight. Set the nails in approximately $1/4$". Now round the ends of the poles. A belt sander works well for this step.

To apply the handles,

take the 14" pole and cut it in half so you have two 7" poles. Round the ends. Sand a flat spot on one side of each pole so you can attach one to each end of the magazine holder. Center the handles, then glue and nail them on. Set the nails in approximately $1/4$". Let the handles dry.

If you are applying a cutout or inlaid piece to the ends of your magazine holder, do that now. Stain and finish only one side of the cutout, or the glue that you use to apply it to the magazine holder will not form a tight bond. Let the stain dry, then glue the cutout or inlaid piece on to the holder.

Finally, rub a tack cloth over the surface of the project to remove any remaining dust, then complete the magazine rack with a finish of your choice.

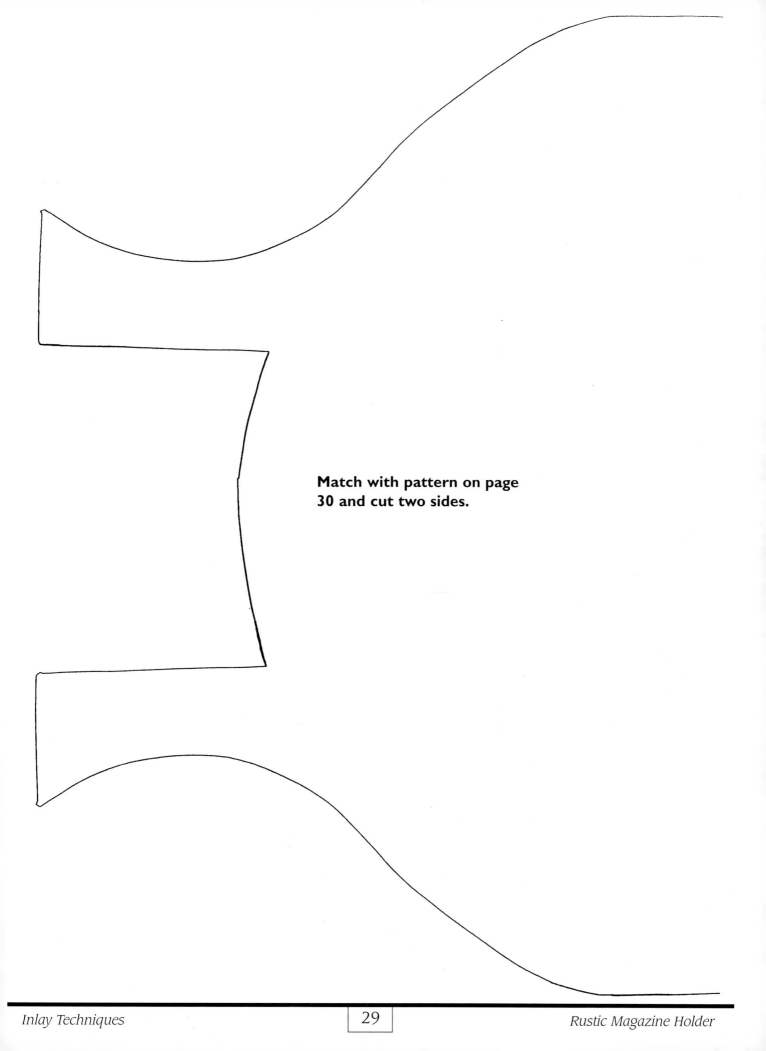

Match with pattern on page 30 and cut two sides.

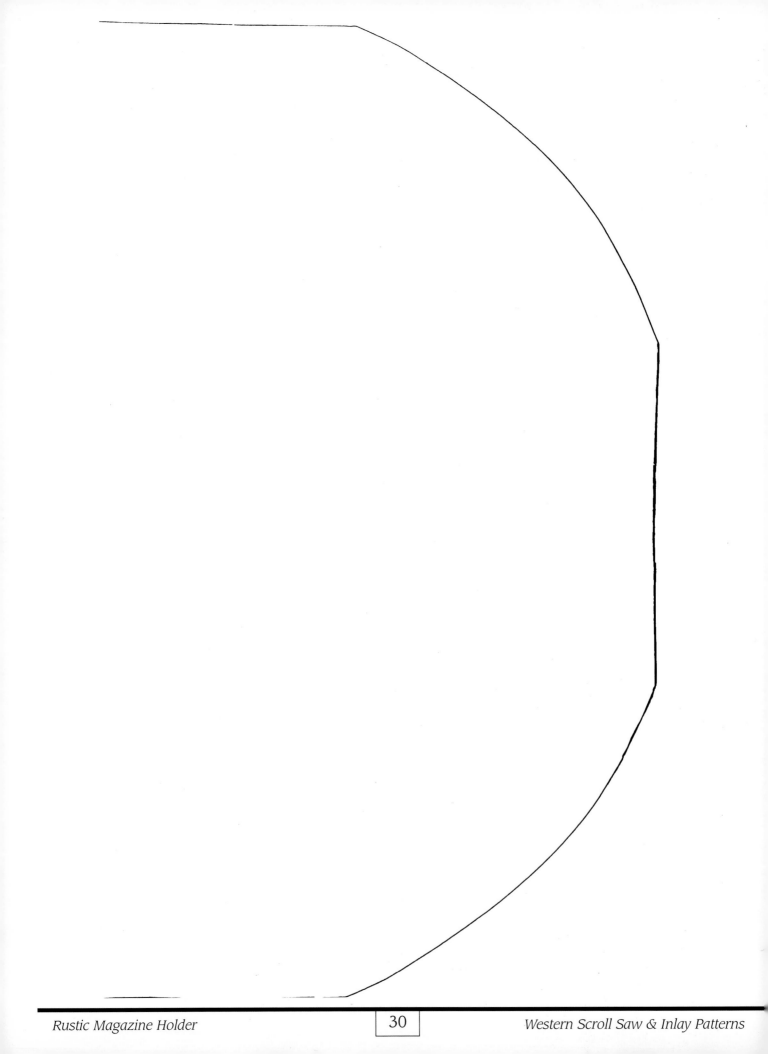

Best Friends

We use these patterns as ornaments, box lids or decrease the size and use them as name tags.

Snowbird

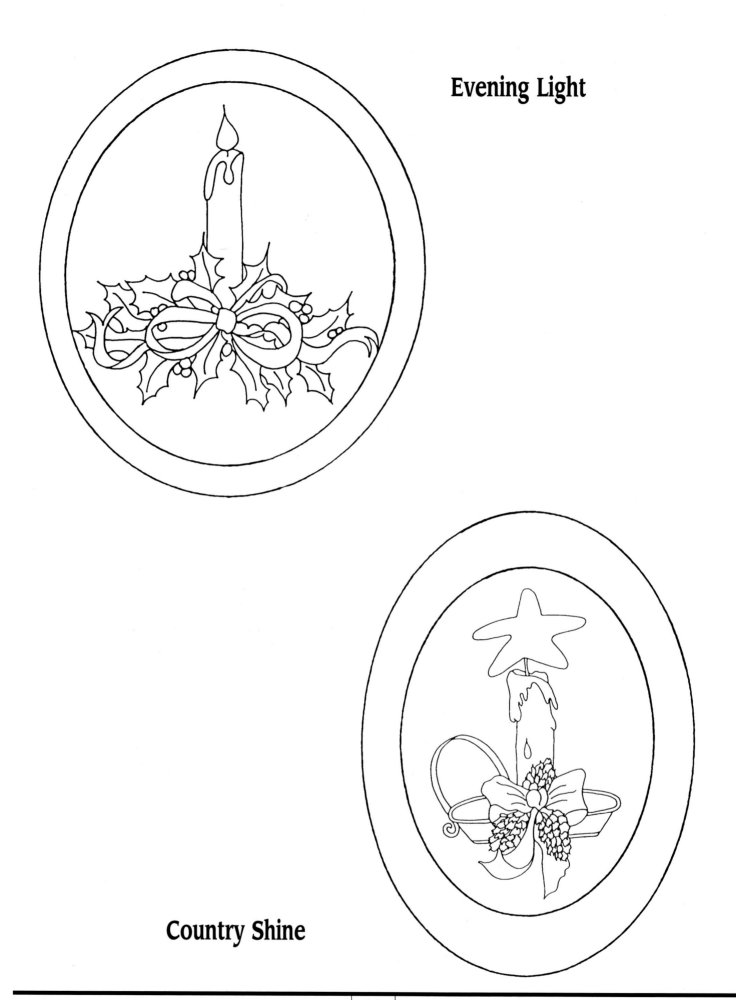

Evening Light

Country Shine

Just a Thought

Christmas Chore

Sheriff

Up Up & Away

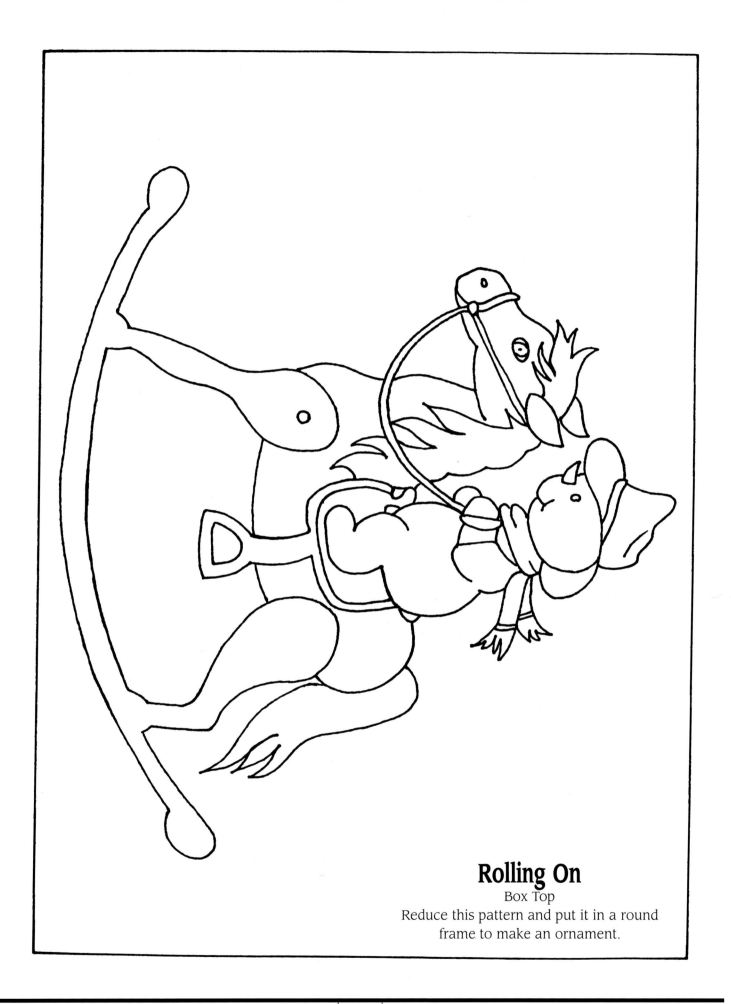

Rolling On
Box Top
Reduce this pattern and put it in a round
frame to make an ornament.

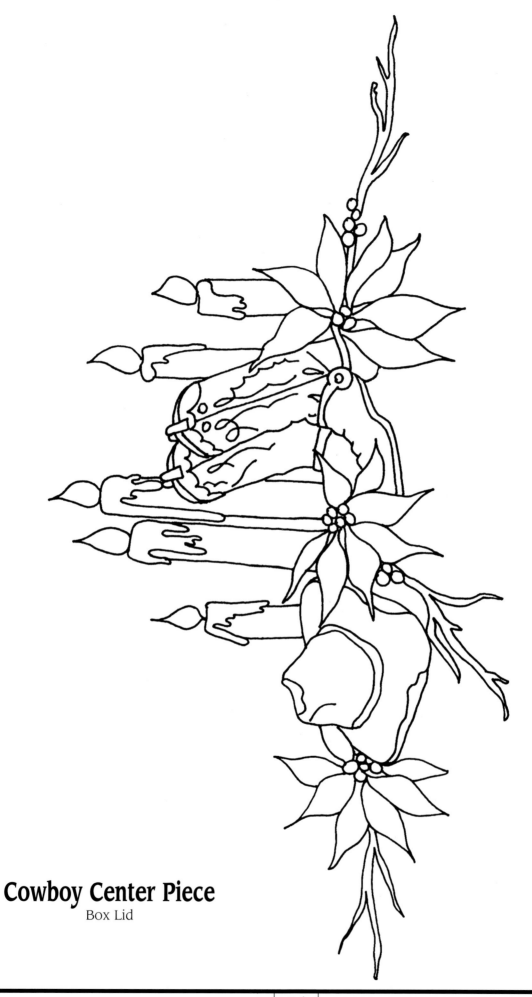

Cowboy Center Piece
Box Lid

Cowboy Santa

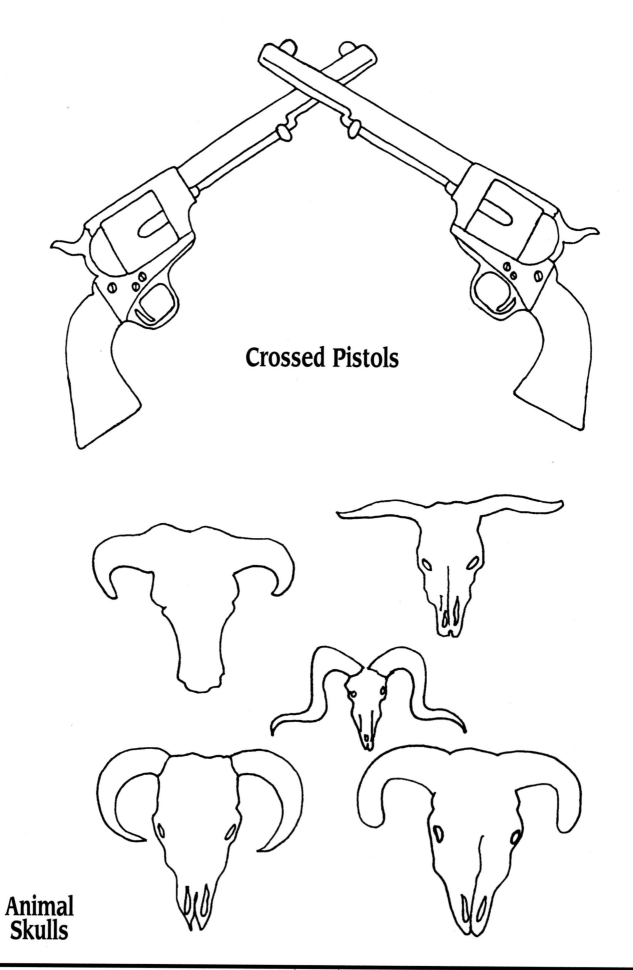

Crossed Pistols

**Animal
Skulls**

Kid Roper

We use these patterns for magnets
and in scenes or for box lids.

Trick Roper

Fence Riders

Heading Home

The Gallop

Cowboy Parking

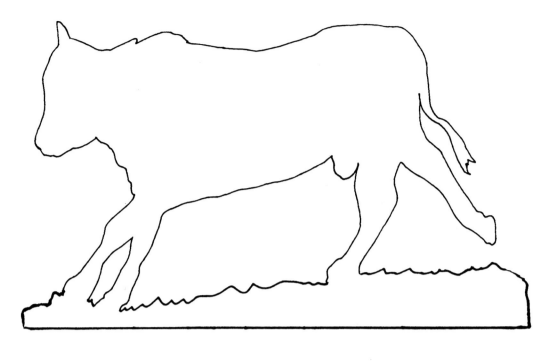

Bull

Antelope

Cowboy Boot

Hats Galore

Wyoming Indian Paintbrush

Country Charm

Silhouette

Cowgirl

Cowboy

Cowgirl Dance

Fence Rider

Bronco

Rough Ride

Barrel Rider

To Work

First Ride

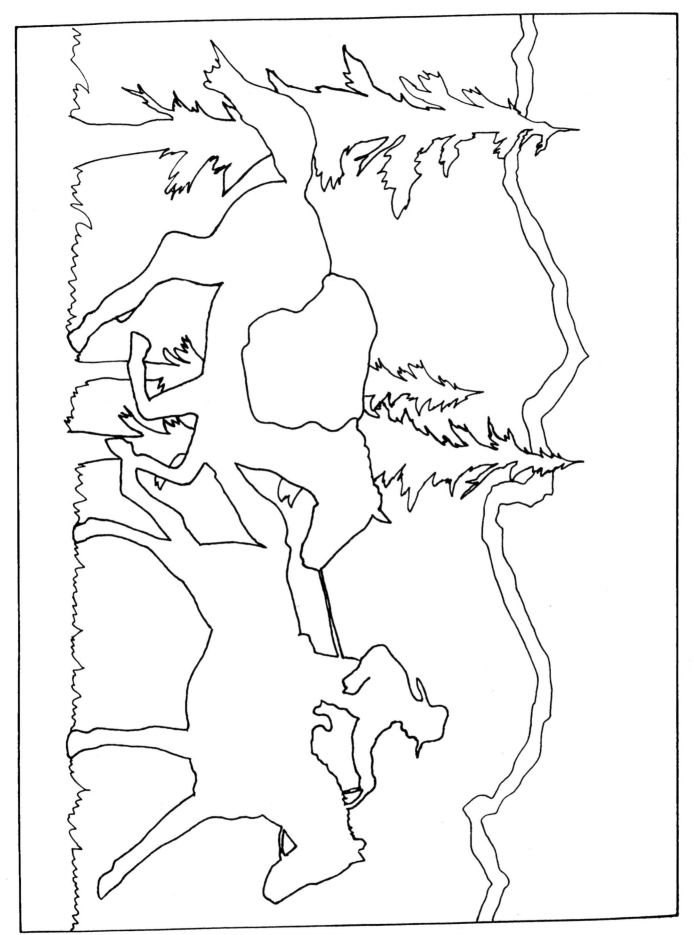

Pack Trip

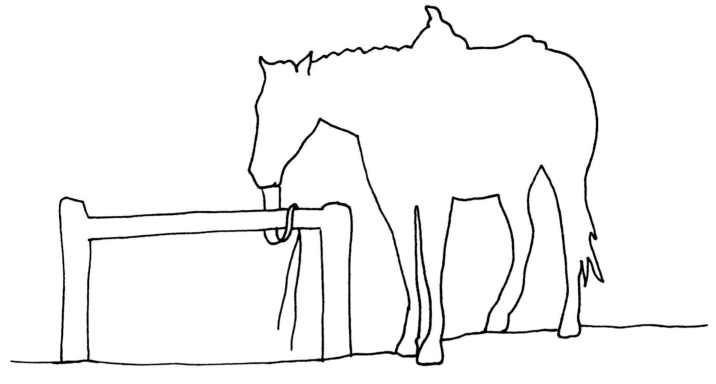

Hitching Post

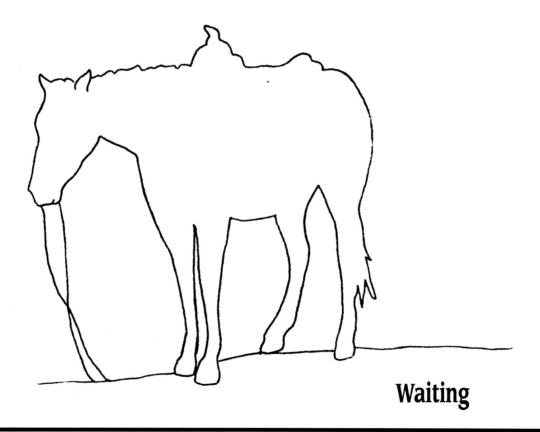

Waiting

Horses

Stallion Pride

Trotting Horse

Colt

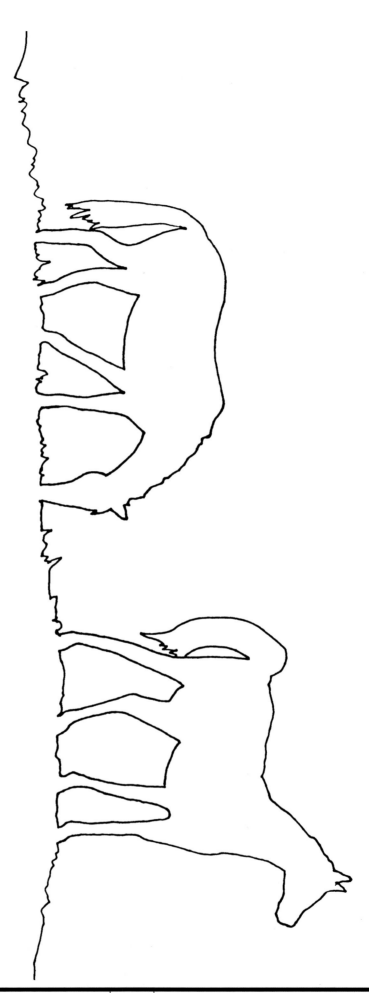

Grazing

Indian Pony

Pony

Picture Perfect.

Curiosity

Colt II

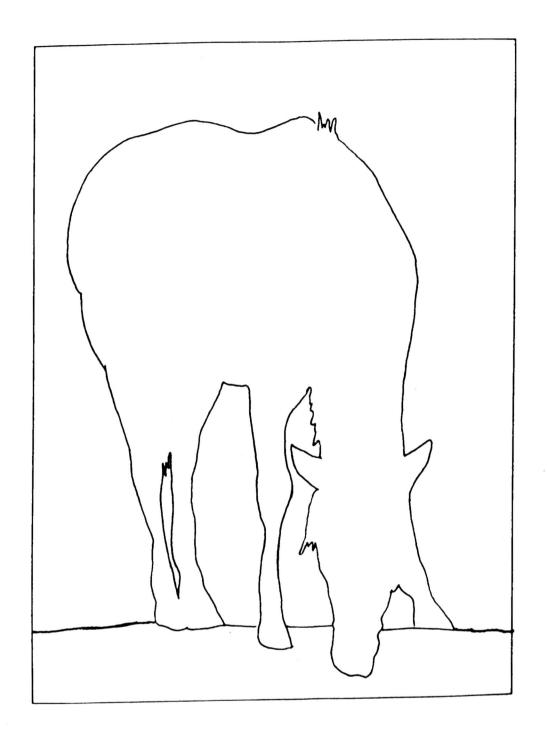

Horse Silhouette

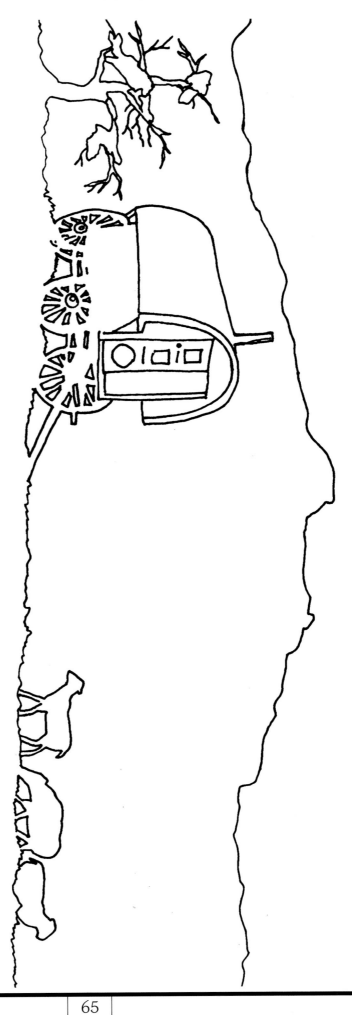

Hart Mountain
(Cody, Wyoming)
Sheep wagon & sheep

Roundup

Bulldogging

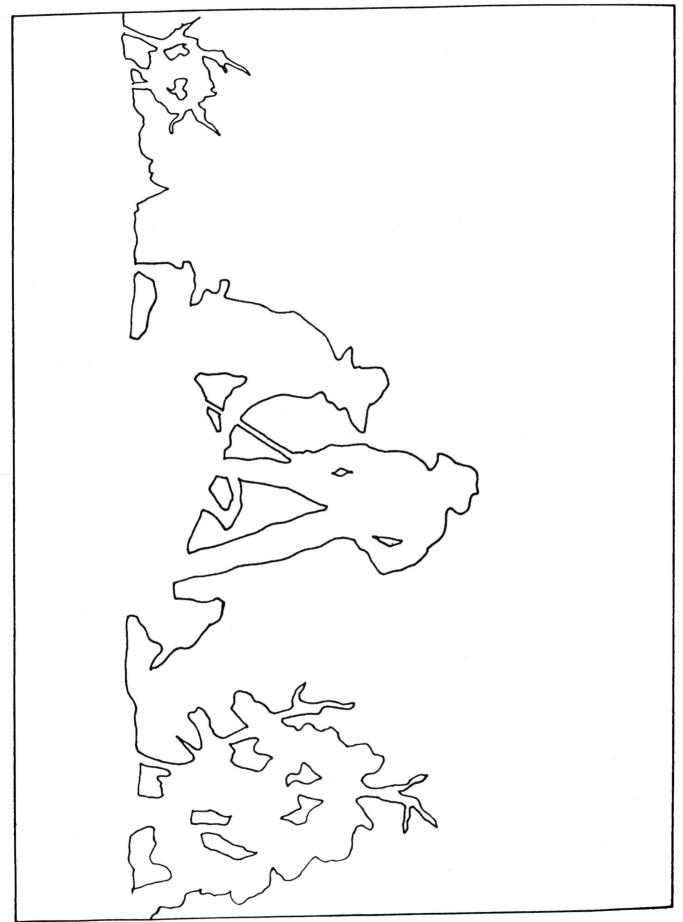

The Branding

The Herd

Shared Space

Mother Cow

Bawling Calf

Cow II

Cow

Buffalo

Buffalo and Baby

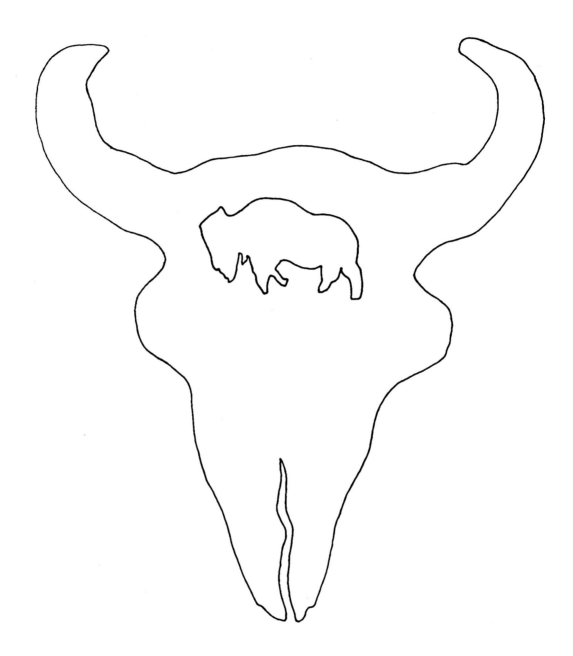

Buffalo Skull with Buffalo

We use these patterns for box lids, magnets,
scenes and inlays.

Mountain Trees.

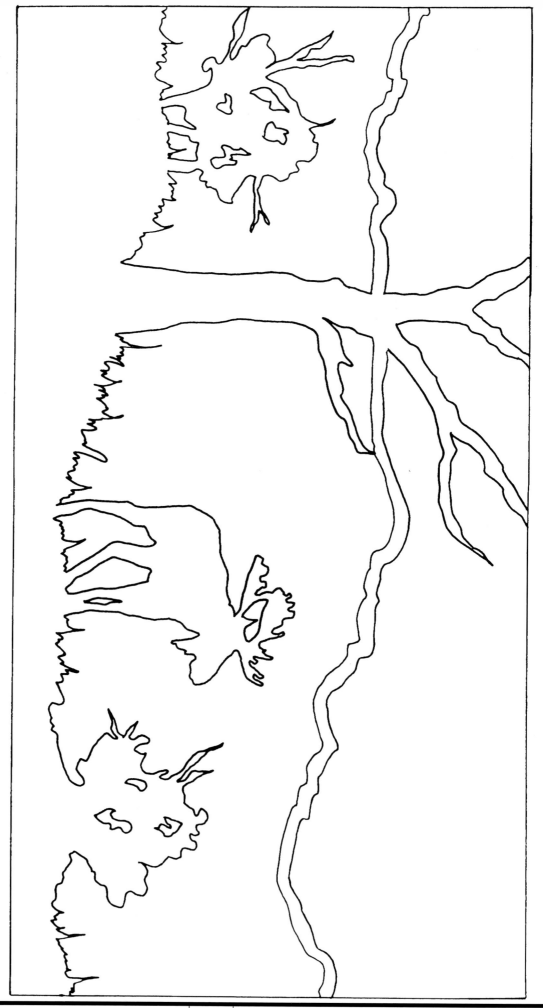

Moose

Cub Bear

Mule Deer

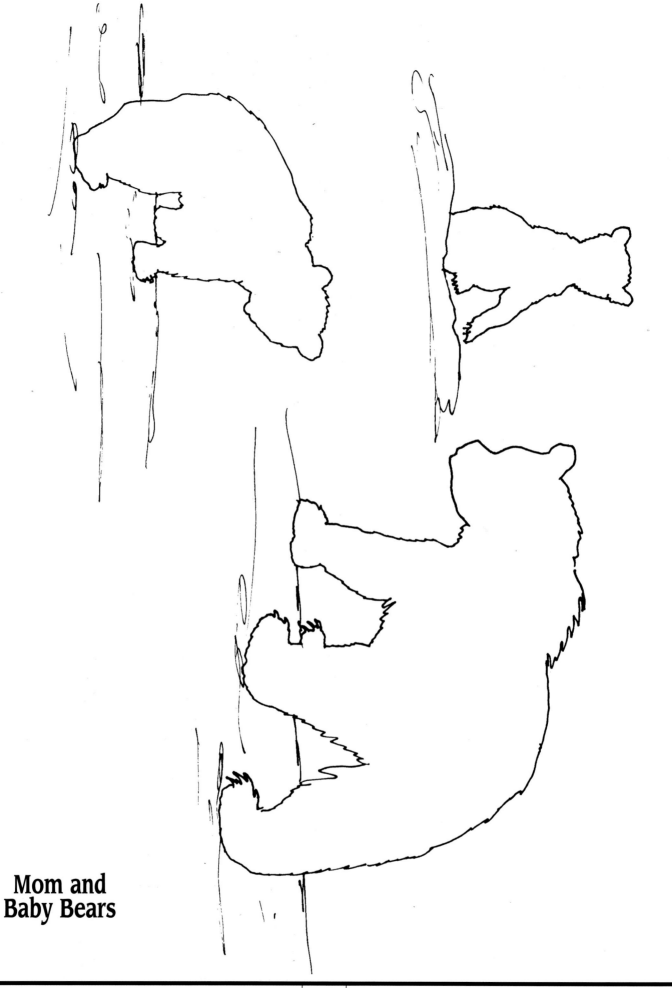

Mom and Baby Bears

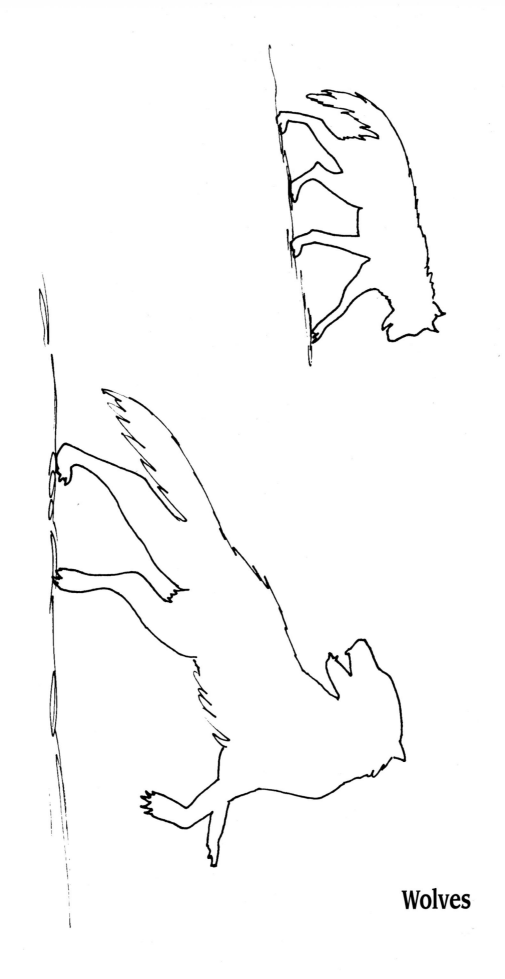

Wolves

Lone Wolf

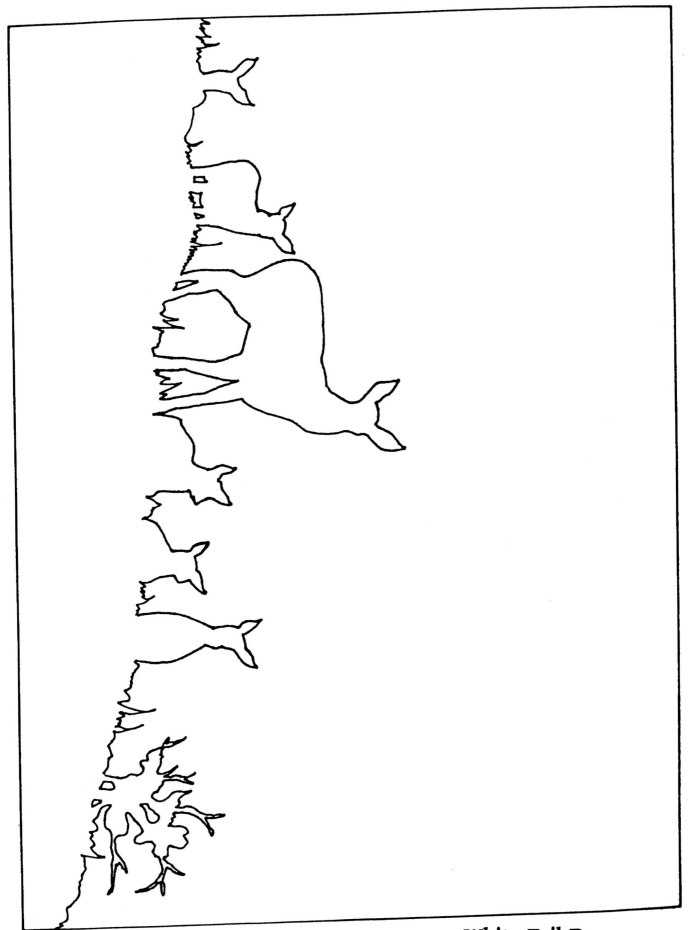

White Tail Deer

Doe and Fawn Deer

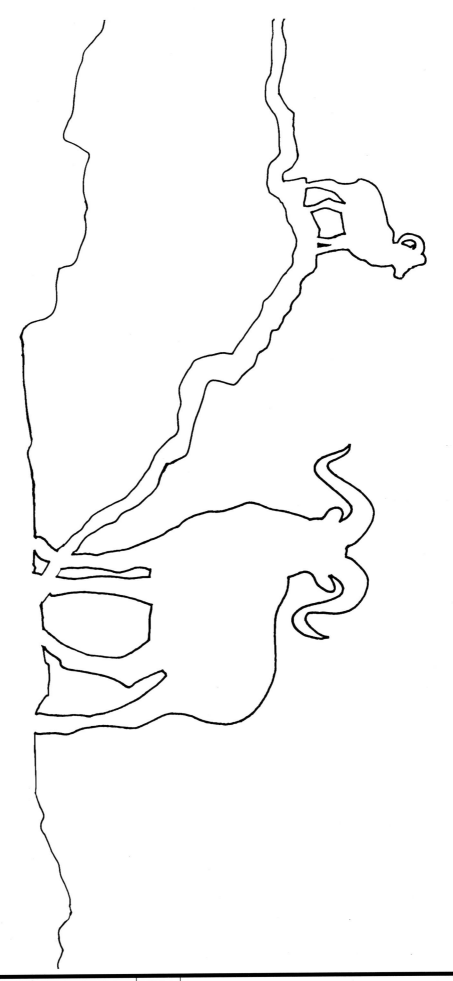

Rocky
Mountain Sheep

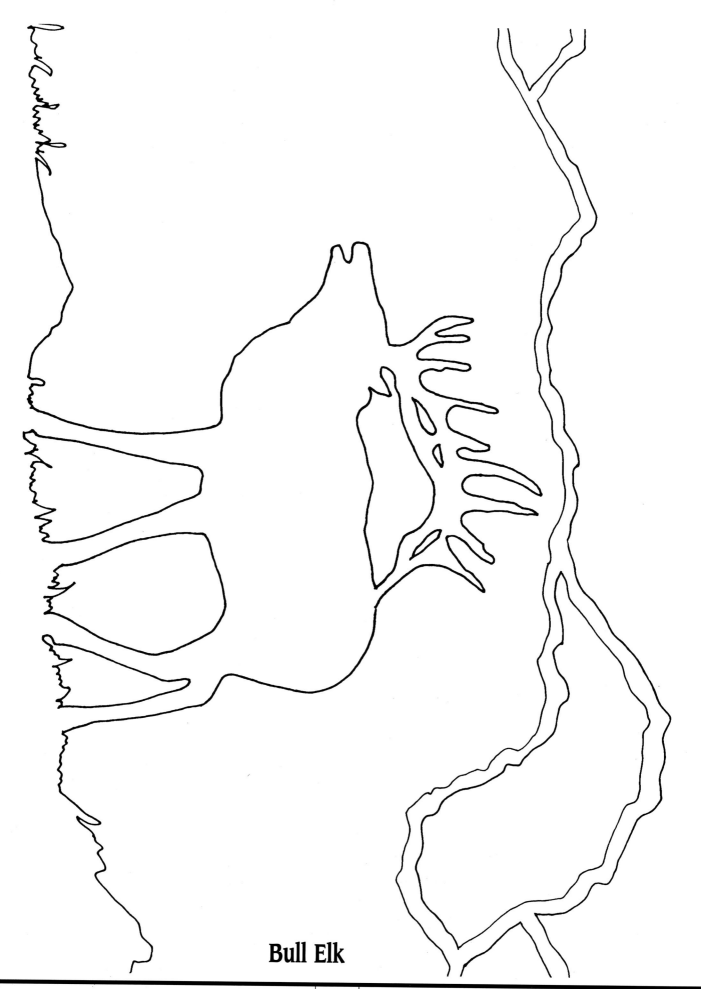

Bull Elk

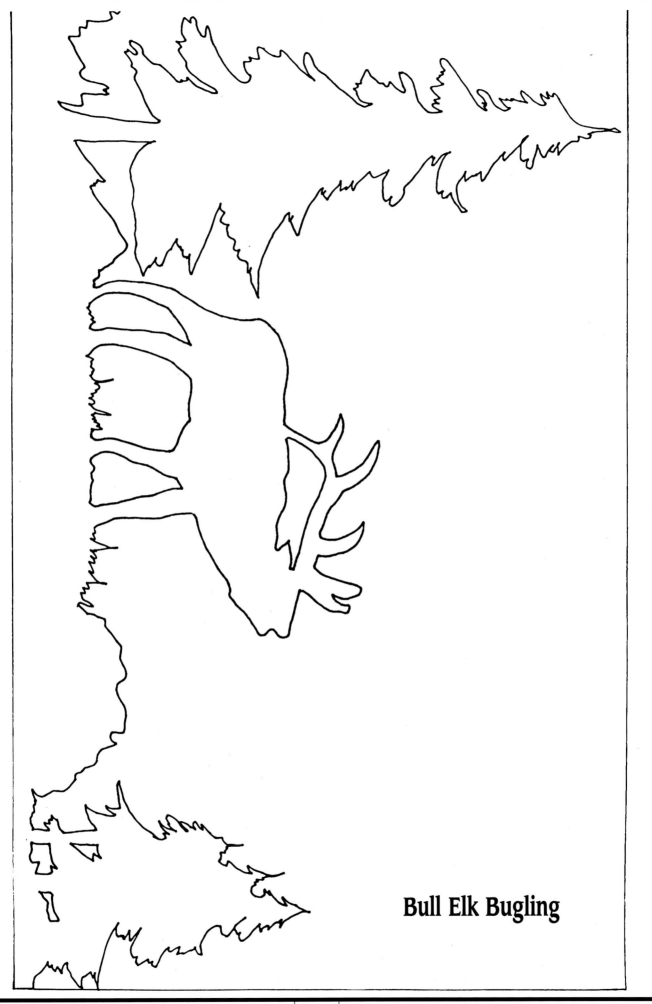

Bull Elk Bugling

CLINTON PUBLIC LIBRARY
CLINTON, IOWA
52732

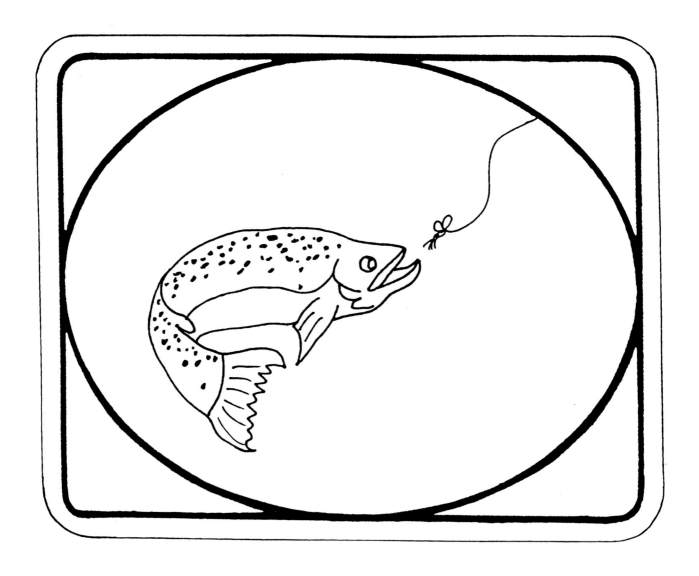

Pretty Fishy

Rainbow Trout

In Flight

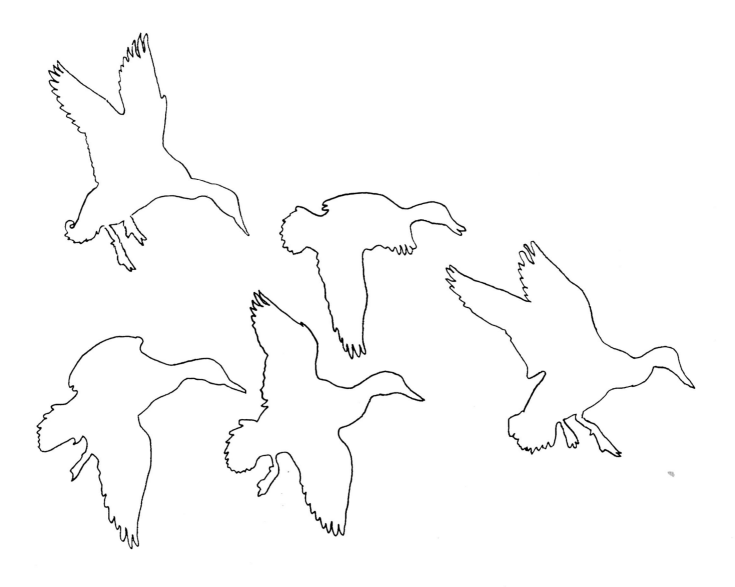

Ducks in Flight

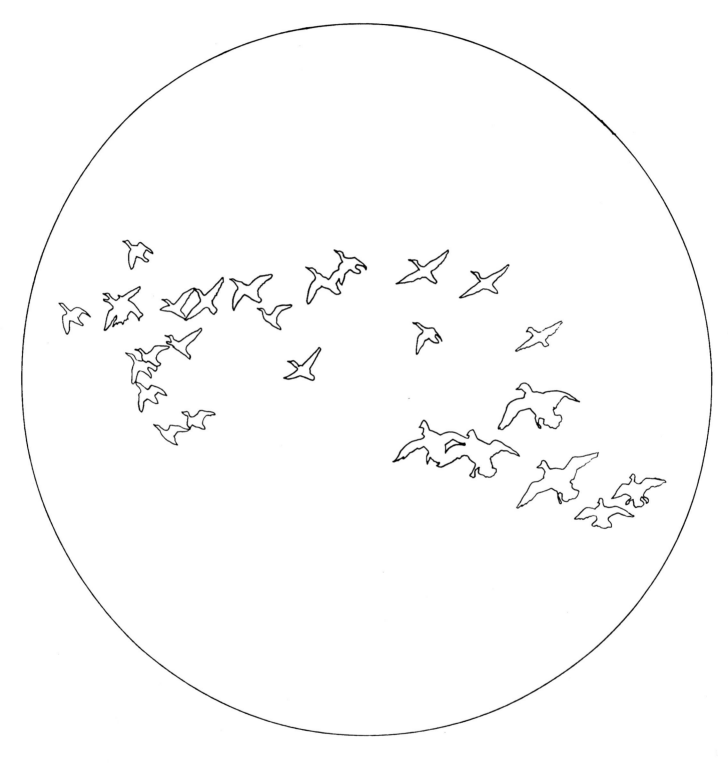

Moonlit Night

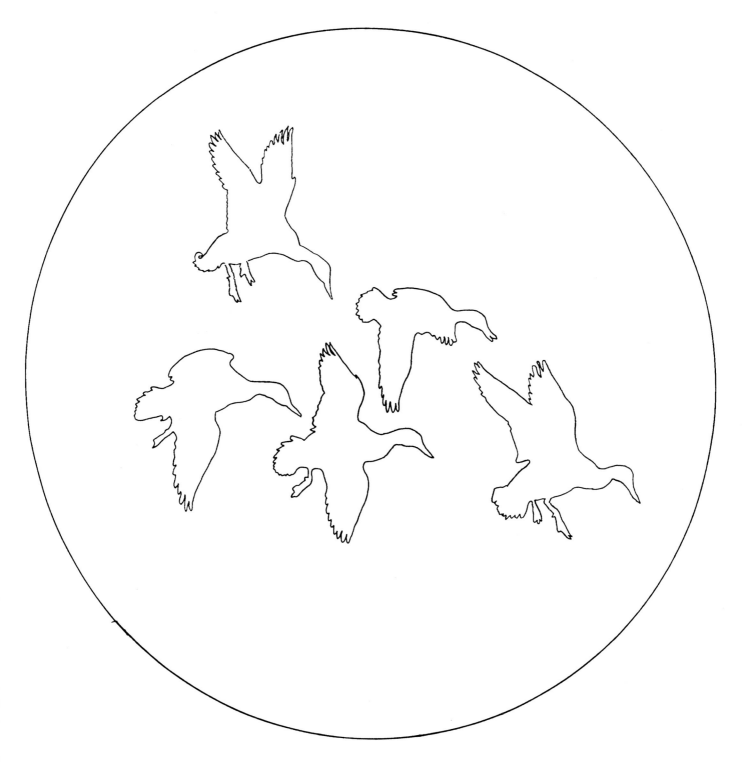

Moonlit Light II

About the Authors

Paige and I have been working together since the day we were married 21 years ago. We have operated Paisley Custom Wood for the past seven years, producing custom lighting, inlaid furniture and accessories for any style of home or office. With 2,000 plus patterns on file, finding one that works is not a problem. We stand by our customers' satisfaction and are dedicated to craftsmanship and creativity. It is nice to own a wood shop that we can be proud of and be able to give our customers the quality product they expect—hand-crafted wood products made one at a time.

—*Joe Paisley*

Paige and Joe can be reached at Paisley Custom Wood, PO Box 488, Meeteetse, WY 82433, (307) 868–2692.